Chav Speak

Crombie Jardine Publishing Limited
13 Nonsuch Walk, Cheam, Surrey, SM2 7LG

www.crombiejardine.com

First published by Crombie Jardine Publishing
Limited in 2004

5th reprint, 2005

ISBN 1-905102-20-8

Concept by Alastair Williams
Design by Rob Smith
Written by Nick Atkinson

Printed and bound in Great Britain by William
Clowes Ltd, Beccles, Suffolk.

Contents

iNtRODUCtiON

WELCOME to the dictionary of Chav speak. It describes and details the extensively limited lexicon of a sociological underclass known to most as 'Chavs'. This growing breed of scallies, charvers and layabouts has gradually developed its own language which is completely unintelligible to the untrained ear.

This book is designed to help the normal English speaker understand the terminology of these groups of people who hang about in shopping centres, leisure parks and bowling alleys in the hope that, through understanding and knowledge, we will one day be able to communicate more efficiently with them.

So next time you walk past a group of Chavs outside a bowling alley, bus station or cinema, try eavesdropping – you may be surprised at what you hear.

tHE LiNGO

a

alloy

noun

'Alloy' describes a mixture of metals, more precious to Chavs than gold. Many Chavs are known to dream about having new wheels for their Novas made from this combination of precious metals.

'ave

verb

Chav speak contraction of the English 'have'. Its use in Chav English is decreasing as the term 'stealed' becomes ever more popular.

arse

noun

Not to be confused with the English word 'ass', meaning 'donkey'. In Chav speak, 'arse' refers to the area of the body from which most Chav speak is uttered.

a'ight

expression / greeting

Used as a greeting, normally coupled with a slack jaw and a swift flick of the fingers.

aun'ie

noun

A kin-term used in Chav speak to describe the female friends of any Chav parent. From an early age Chav parents confuse their children's understanding of kin-terms by encouraging the presence of such fictitious 'aun'ies'.

baaastard

noun

An insult – often used when a Chav is caught out by the DSS for benefit fraud or their neighbour sends the environmental health round to their house to investigate the stench.

beauty

adjective

A euphemistic term falling out of use as in-breeding takes over in Chav communities leading to a mass ugliness epidemic. The only current use evident in Chav speak is when a speaker is referring to a set of recently stolen hub caps that actually looks the same as alloy wheels.

bench

noun

'Benches' are found outside bowling alleys, cinemas, and amusement arcades in every town centre or leisure complex in the country. No true Chavs can afford to enter any of these establishments and thus are grateful to local councils for giving them somewhere to sit and abuse the public.

bo

adjective

'Bo' is used in Chav speak for expressing the positive qualities of any item. For emphasis can be preceded by 'well' or 'proper'. Also refers to the smell emanating from armpits.

bill

noun

Another spectre of Chav mythology. Rumour has it that bills must be paid in order to receive goods and services. However, any self-respecting Chav knows that it is more cost-effective to get rehoused than to pay up.

bollocks

noun / adjective

i) The male genitalia.

ii) The term used to describe something as awful, particularly car stereos, stolen TVs or clothes that are unbranded.

brother

noun

i) The person any self-respecting Chavette desires to wed.

ii) A sibling of the same parents – the identity of whom is often unknown.

bucket

noun

A cheap way for a Chav to consume 'weed'. The Chav saves on tobacco and Rizlas by adopting this D.I.Y. approach to drug consumption.

Chav

noun / verb

i) *Noun*. The manifested humanitarian equivalent to either stepping on an upturned plug or having chewing gum stuck to your shoe.

ii) *Verb*. To steal.

Chavette

noun

The female equivalent of a Chav
except with more hair mousse, a
shorter skirt and a deeper voice.
Chavettes can be found in their
natural habitat hanging around
bus stops, shopping malls and in
fast food restaurants.

cousin

noun

A person ripe for marrying. At least if they look like you, you can recognise them in a crowd and you know in advance what the kids will look like.

24

cunt

noun / adjective

i) *Noun.* The female genitalia.

ii) *Adjective.* Used to describe a person who impedes the smooth existence of a Chav in any way. This may be done by simply being alive, having expensive trainers or being over 16 and not having a baby.

cushdy

adjective

An expression coined in a classic British television comedy, with origins in Cockney English. In Chav speak it is used to describe a positive event such as winning £1.00 on a scratch card or getting a new keyring for your Nova that bears the Ferrari logo.

D

dealer

noun

A person who supplies illegal drugs, usually affording himself high status within Chav society. Respected and loved by Chavs and their parents everywhere.

dat

pronoun

Used in place of the English 'that'. Normally used to point out another person's property, such as any car registered later than 1984 or the stereo contained within said car. Mutually interchangeable with 'vat' or 'nat'.

dis

preposition

Hip-hop Chav speak for the English term 'this'. Linguists argue that this is simply an example of language change in modern society. The truth, however, is that Chavs just don't talk properly.

diss

verb

A contraction of the English term 'disrespect'. 'Dissing' a Chav / Chavette is easy and will frustrate him / her greatly as he / she will not be able think fast enough to come up with a response. Some excellent 'disses' to be used on Chavs are:

- You look like your mum.

- Your signet ring isn't from Argos.

- Your dad hasn't been to prison.

- Your trainers look old.

- Why do your trainers have four stripes?

- Why can your family breathe under water and swim really fast? (Referring to the gills and webbing that have evolved out of repeated inbreeding.)

dog

adjective / noun

i) *Adjective.* Derogatory term. A Chav may describe his girlfriend, mother or the mother of his child as being 'dog' ugly.

ii) *Noun.* A canine pet employed by Chavs nationwide in order to gain extra benefit from the DSS.

e

easy

adjective

Used to describe any Chavette regarded by Chav society as being over-willing to conduct sexual relations with just about anybody.

easy now

greeting

Friendly introduction used only between Chavs. Can be followed by many words, the choice of which reflects the speaker's opinion of the recipient. Examples include 'bad boy', 'gangster', 'playa' and 'soldier'.

F

fags

noun

i) People of homosexual origin. If you are gay, never let this fact be revealed to a Chav. He will try to give you a shoeing because he is very much afraid of you.

ii) Cigarettes.

father

noun

A creature out of Chav mythology often spoke of, but never seen - what Chavs become when they die / disappear / go to prison.

fingerprint

noun

Used in place of 'signature' in Chav speak. Chavs are more commonly required to sign their name in this way than with a pen. Most Chavs cannot write anyway.

fit

adjective

'Fit' is used in an unconventional sense in Chav speak. Its meaning bears little resemblance to the English form. For a Chav / Chavette to call someone 'fit', the subject must be 'well frosted', have 'nuff bling' and definitely be 'phat'.

flex

noun

Most commonly used in the phrase 'What's the flex?' This has the same meaning as the English phrase 'What's going on?' Only it's not the same, because it is 'wack'.

flexing

verb

If you are 'flexing' a Chav, you are more than likely annoying him / her because to 'flex' is to insult or frustrate. 'Flexing' a Chav is easily done by asking simple maths questions, asking them to spell anything or write their own name without using just the symbol 'x'.

frosted

adjective

Describes the status of one's 'bling'. If one's bling is 'well frosted', it is assumed to be voluminous in quantity, usually meaning that you have 'nuff gold' or a signet ring wiv a real pound coin in.

41

fuck

expletive

This English taboo word is encouraged in Chav speak and should be used regularly and with much bravado. (E.g. 'What the fuckin' fuck is fuckin' 'appenin' wiv your fuckin' bling – it was nuff frosted but now it's fuckin' wack, innit?')

G

gangster

noun

The pinnacle of Chav ambition; a career path providing status, consumables and respect. Being a 'gangster' offers Chavs the chance to live an existence outside of the law. A bit like all other Chavs, really.

geek

noun

Used by Chavs as a term of respect for people more intelligent than themselves. People can qualify as a 'geek' in the eyes of any Chav in many ways. These range from knowing how to tie their own shoelaces, to wearing glasses or not smoking.

grass

verb / noun

i) *Verb*. Used to refer to the act of reporting any crime to the police or anyone in authority.

ii) *Noun*. The person who committed the act of 'grassing'. Being a grass almost certainly guarantees being beaten up.

iii) *Noun*. Marijuana.

H

hat

noun

A popular fashion accessory worn by most Chavs to conceal their identity from CCTV cameras in petrol stations, shopping centres, football stadiums and prison line-ups across the country.

i

innit

tag question

Contraction of the English 'isn't it?'
An extremely popular expression
used by Chavs at the end of
'sentences' in order to qualify their
previous statement. An example of
this phenomenon is 'Dat stereo is
well phat, innit?'

joint

noun

The preferred method of consuming marijuana used by Chavs. This option is only available when tobacco and Rizlas can be afforded, usually on benefit day.

joyride

noun / verb

When a Chav procures another person's vehicle with the intention of doing handbrake turns and wheelspins in the car park of any garden centre or supermarket, he or she can be said to be 'joyriding'.

49

k

kicking

noun

Used by Chavs in place of the English 'fight'. 'Kickings' are either given or received by Chavs. In both instances it usually involves someone younger than the Chav.

knob

noun

i) The male genitalia. Commonly found growing from the foreheads of most Chavs.

ii) An insult.

iii) A household fixing that must be forced in order for Chavs to successfully burgle your house.

51

large

adjective

In Chav speak, when something is said to be 'large' it not only refers to the physical size of the object in question, but also describes the object as being rather good. Thus it is unlikely that however fat a Chavette gets, she will ever be 'large'.

lemon

noun

When a recently purchased Nova saloon proves to have sawdust in the engine, no exhaust pipe and is held together by rust, in Chav speak it can be said to be a 'lemon'.

lies

noun

The Chav speak equivalent of the English term 'truth'. 'Lies' are used by Chavs in a number of situations such as police questioning, teacher interrogation and during paternity tests. Apparently daytime TV diva 'Trisha' has invented a foolproof 'lie detector test' to spot any Chav 'truths'.

life

noun

What some Chavs end up getting, courtesy of any sane-minded judge, for any combination of road-traffic offences, dole fraud or fashion crimes.

luv

noun

A sexual emotion shared between a Chav and his Nova or a Chavette and her hair mousse. Similar to the English term 'love' but spelt differently and of a more sexual orientation.

man

noun

The correct way to finish any well constructed sentence in Chav speak, innit man.

massive

noun

In Chav speak, unlike in English, the term 'massive' is a noun, not an adjective. Chavs are not massive, rather a 'massive' is something that is 'had'. It refers to a large collection of Chavs, usually found loitering with intent around cash machines, leisure complexes and scrap-yards.

me

pronoun

Chav speak form of the English 'my'. For example 'Me trainers are well phat'.

microwave

noun

Item found in every Chav kitchen in the country. All meals in Chav households are prepared using this technological wonder. Apparently you put cold food in for 30 seconds and it comes out hot enough to melt steel. Believe.

mint

adjective

Euphemism used to describe the condition of a recently purchased / stolen Nova saloon or Mk2 Fiesta. If said vehicle comes equipped with either neon underlighting or blacked-out windows, it can be said to be 'well mint'.

minger

noun

A euphemistic term to describe the more beautiful of the Chavettes. The antonym of 'minger' is 'absolute disgrace'. Examples of mingers in society are Posh Spice, Jade and Jordan.

money

noun

Another legend from Chav mythology. Money is thought to be 'rarer than gold' by most Chavs and although freely dispersed by the DSS on production of your ration book, most Chavs will never know what it is like to hold a real £20 note.

mother

noun

The first lady of the Chav household. She is often found whiling away the days watching daytime TV in her dressing gown, yelling at the little Chavs, and smoking 60+ cigarettes a day. Defining characteristics are: i) a penchant for smoking; ii) being single; iii) a love of TV-related magazines.

motor

noun

Used in Chav speak to refer to any car that has been 'enhanced' with plastic body kits, stick-on 'carbon fibre' accessories or go-faster stripes. The true Chav will always have a 'motor', whether it has an MOT or not.

naff

adjective

A dying expression favoured by Chavs in the late '90s to describe something that isn't 'mint', 'phat', 'large' or 'bo'.

nah

particle

Same as English 'no'. Used most commonly as a direct response to the questions, 'Is that your baby?', 'Do you live here?' or 'Have you been in paid employment in the past 365 days?'

nick

noun / verb

i) *Noun*. Refers to the English term 'prison'. A place where many Chav families have been known to spend Christmas or meet up with long lost relatives.

ii) *Verb*. To steal.

nuff

adjective

A mutated version of the English 'enough', used by Chavs in place of the English intensifier 'really'. So in Chav speak, your bling is not 'really frosted' but in fact 'nuff frosted'.

nuffink

adverb

Can be used interchangeably in place of either 'anything' or 'nothing'. 'Nuffink' is a term usually used by Chavs in conjunction with the verbs 'got', 'have' and 'done'.

o

open

adjective

An important term in Chav speak, used as an excuse when confronted by the police, a homeowner or an ex-girlfriend's parents.

E.g. 'The door was already open' or 'Her legs just opened'.

pap

adjective

Derogatory term used to describe any object, event or place that falls below the inflated expectations of a Chav. An example might be 'Southend is pap'.

phat

adjective

Euphemistic term used in Chav speak to describe the width of a gold chain, the quality of a pair of new Nike Air or the girth of a Chavette.

poor

adjective

The social status most Chavs aspire to being. It is easily obtainable, doesn't involve work and the DSS gives you money.

proper

adjective

An adjective to be used anywhere in a sentence to intensify another adjective. (E.g. 'My signet ring is proper phat, innit man.')

Q

quit

verb

What Chavs do after twenty minutes in any type of gainful employment.

razz

verb

To drive one's vehicle excessively fast around school playgrounds, market squares or car parks. Chav people can also 'razz', especially when being chased by dealers, the police or the DSS.

refrigerator

noun

Classed in English as 'white goods'. In Chav speak, however, the term 'stolen goods' is more appropriate. Used for keeping energy drinks cold.

ruff

adjective

i) Derogatory term used to describe the physical state of Posh Spice or most Chavettes.

ii) Euphemistic term used to describe the 'phatness' of the bass levels offered by one's stereo system.

iii) The noise a dog makes.

rights

noun

'Rights' are read to Chavs from a very early age, usually by policemen or parents who don't know any bedtime stories.

safe

adjective

When a Chav robs your house and takes your TV, video and Playstation and escapes, not only should you have put the items in a safe, the Chav is the one that is now truly 'safe'. (Unless the police have caught his cap-wearing behind and thrown him in the 'nick' with the rest of his family.)

scally

noun

Thanks to a lack of birth control, Scallies are a growing breed of Chav, found mainly in the North West. Their specialist skills include burglary, abusing old people, making babies smoke and stealing hub caps.

skank

noun

Every Chav is a skank: someone who always wants something for nothing and is more than prepared to steal if needs must. The noun 'skank' is not to be confused with the verb 'skanking' which is a popular form of dancehall music.

Sharon

name

The favoured name of most Chavettes, especially when naming their daughters after themselves.

sharp

adjective

A descriptive term used to describe a Chav who is wearing brand new white trainers, the latest Nickelson pastel-coloured polo shirt and freshly ironed 3-stripe tracksuit bottoms. That outfit would make anybody look 'sharp'.

shite

noun / adjective

i) *Noun*. Excrement.

ii) *Adjective*. Term used to describe how 'pap' something is. (E.g. 'That motor is fuckin' shite, innit man'.)

shop-lifting

noun

A favoured hobby / job of most Chavs. It is a route to clothing and feeding your child, prison and missing school and thus is a highly respected activity in Chav communities.

signet

noun

Not to be confused with 'signature', 'signet' is a type of grotesque finger jewellery worn by the more well-to-do male Chav. If the owner is particularly wealthy it may contain a real pound coin as its centrepiece or be engraved with the word 'phat'.

sorted

adjective

When a crime is successfully carried out and a new packet of nappies or a new signet ring is in the sticky hands of the Chav, things are said to be 'sorted'.

squark

sound

The high pitch vocalisation made by a Chavette, when in mating season. This happens every Tuesday night when the bowling alley shuts early.

shoeing

adjective

The Chav speak term for 'beating somebody up'. If a 'shoeing' is dealt out by a Chav, it will never hurt because the soles of their shoes are always made of air and thus soft to the touch.

†

tax

verb

Meaning to steal. This term should not be confused with the English 'tax' as the only 'tax' that Chavs pay is that which the government levies on their cigarettes. Paying income tax entails having a job and paying council tax entails having a house.

twister

noun

Anyone who messes with the mind of a Chav by demanding simple motor-neurone skills such as adding, subtracting, reading or writing. Most teachers are thought to be 'twisters'.

TMC

acronym

'TMC' stands for 'Totally Mint Condition'. The term is used to describe any rust-free Nova saloon, Fiesta or Escort XR3i.

TWOC

acronym

Taken Without Owner's Consent. Legal jargon designed to confuse simple-minded Chavs. Only found in Chav speak because of the massive numbers of Chavs that have been exposed to the term while being arrested for nicking.

television

noun

The favourite possession of most Chav parents. Up to 24 hours a day can be spent watching television by the more committed enthusiasts and owners of satellite dishes. Televisions can also be stolen and traded in pubs for money or wheel trims.

ugly

adjective

A word used to describe the facial characteristics of most Chavs and Chavettes. Unlike the story of 'The Ugly Duckling', most Chavs cannot hope to blossom into beautiful swans, although they have a similar life expectancy.

V

vat

pronoun

Chav speak form of the English 'that'. Used referentially by Chavs to point things out in time and space. (E.g. 'Vat motor is bling.')

W

wack

adjective

When something is 'shite', it is also, by definition, 'wack' and vice versa. Trainers that aren't white are 'wack', as are jobs, fathers, teachers and shirts that don't bare the cross of St George.

wa g'wan

phrase

'Wa g'wan' is a contraction of the
English phrase 'What is going on?'
In Chav speak it is a 'hip-hop' term
of greeting.

washing machine

noun

An item referred to in Chav mythology. Used for making your socks and England shirts whiter than white. 'Washing machines' are found in laundrettes across the country but rumour has it that soon they will be affordable enough for residential purchase.

Wayne

name

'Wayne' is the Chav speak equivalent of the English term 'Jesus'. Chav parents name all of their male children 'Wayne' in the hope that he will be the next 'chosen one' and possibly make it to the promised land known as 'the college'.

well

intensifier

Used in Chav speak in place of the English term 'really'. Anything can be 'well' good, 'well' bad, 'well' large or 'well' phat. Chavettes are 'well' phat.

wheel-trims

noun

Wheel-trims are used by Chavs as a form of currency, to trade for various goods and services. The advantages of using them instead of money are that they are more easily obtainable than money, there is a greater range of denominations (based around a variety of styles) and they are big so you can't lose them.

wiv

preposition

Mutation of the English term 'with'. When a Chavette is the girlfriend of a Chav (or pregnant by him), she can be said to be 'wiv' him. It is similar in meaning to the English expression 'the partner of'.

X

Don't be ridiculous. Chav's don't know any words beginning with x.

Y

yellow newspapers

noun

These advertising newspapers are treated as both books and catalogues by Chavs. All Christmas shopping is done with the aid of such retail bibles. It is possible to obtain almost any item you can imagine for under £5.00. This includes cars.

yo

greeting

A greeting between Chavs that can be repeated as many times as the speaker wishes. In fact it might be suggested that two 'yo's' are better than one. E.g. 'Yo. Yo yo. Yo yo yo. Yo yo yo yo'.

Z

See X, although it is tempting to include the word 'Zebra', just for posterity.

CHAV JOKE₂:

How would you describe a Chav who's fallen in the river?

iNNit.

What word best describes a Chav in a filing box?

ZORteD.

What do you call a Chav who gets accidentally locked in a bank vault?

Zafe.

What do you call a Chav who eats a lot of fish, wears fur and lives in an igloo?

iNNuiNNit.

What do Chavs and slinkies have in common?

There's plenty of fun to be had watching them fall down some very steep ƨɈɒiᴙƨ.

If two Chavs are in a car and there's no music blaring, then who's doing the driving?

tHE PoLiCE.

What's the descriptive term for a Chavette wearing a white tracksuit?

tHe BRiDe.

Despite the temptation it's best not to run over a Chav on a bike when you're driving. Why?

It's probably your Bike he's riding.

What are the first words of a baby Chav to its beloved single parent?

WHat you Lookin' at?

What's the difference between a Chavette and a sheep?

One's so stupid it will follow without thinking, wallow in dirt and get rutted without noticing; the other's a ƧHЄЄρ.

How does a Chavette turn off the light after sex?

She closes the car DOOR.

CHAV CHat-ups.

1. Kiss me or I'll make you touch me spots.

2. You've never known true filth until you've kissed me.

3. My cousin loaned me his Nova for just one night – wanna go for a ride?

4. Wanna help me make ugly children?

5. I love the way your belly spills over your tracksuit bottoms – can I touch it?

6. Let's get together and make sweet R 'n' B.

7. Come back to mine and see me collection of signet rings.

8. Kiss me or I'll lamp you.

9. Can I park me Nova in your garage?

10. Get your tracksuit top girl, coz you've pulled.

The Little Book of

Wanking

The definitive guide to man's ultimate relief

DICK PALMER

ISBN 1-905102-00-3, £2.99

ISBN 1-905102-03-8, £2.99

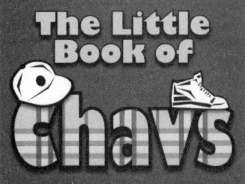

The Little Book of Chavs

The Branded Guide to Britain's New Elite

LEE BOK

ISBN 1-905102-01-1, £2.99

www.crombiejardine.com